Colour Therapy

GW00691463

Vijaya Kumar

NEW DAWN PRESS, INC.
Chicago • Slough • New Delhi

NEW DAWN PRESS GROUP

Published by New Dawn Press Group
New Dawn Press, Inc., 244 South Randall Rd # 90, Elgin, IL 60123

New Dawn Press, 2 Tintern Close, Slough, Berkshire, SL1-2TB, UK

New Dawn Press (An Imprint of Sterling Publishers (P) Ltd.)
A-59, Okhla Industrial Area, Phase-II, New Delhi-110020

Colour Therapy
Copyright © 2004, New Dawn Press
ISBN 1 932705 19 8

NOTE FROM THE PUBLISHER

*The author specifically disclaims any liability, loss or risk
whatsoever, which is incurred or likely to be incurred, as a
consequence of any direct or indirect use of information given
in this book. The contents of this work are a personal
interpretation of the subject by the author.*

PRINTED IN INDIA

Contents

Introduction

Red as a beetroot ... a yellow streak ... green with envy ... having the blues ... white as snow ... in the pink ... the list can go on – showing that colours are very much a part of our lives and health. Colours are present in all walks of life, everywhere and anywhere.

Colour influences our energy system by its vibrations, affecting both our physical and emotional well-being. By using the right colours, we can change our negative aspects into positive ones, be healthier, and acquire a higher level of consciousness. Colour therapy helps to balance the frequencies of malfunctioning cells, and to bounce back to our natural state of radiant well-being. This book tells you how the changing colours around you, and energy come together to create happiness, health, greater abundance, and therapeutic benefits.

Colour Basics

- In the strictest sense, there are actually only three primary colours: red, green and blue–violet (not to be confused with the three primary used in painting and printing — red, yellow and blue).
- These three primary colours in light — red, blue and green, when mixed together in proper proportions result in white light.
- The combination of any two colours gives complementary colour to the third. For e.g. red and light green produce yellow which is complementary to blue-violet.
- Our bodies select from the sunlight whatever colours are needed for maintaining the correct balance, the corresponding or respective vibrations being absorbed into us.
- This process can be seen in the aura around us, and can be photographed through the kiritian technique or high-voltage photography.
- It is a proven fact that even without vision, the body reacts to light or senses light possibly because the skin senses radiation through certain cells.

- The principle underlying the concept of healing with colours is to give the ailing body an added dose of any colour that is lacking.
- The red end of the spectrum stimulates, while the blue end calms, as it has a cooling and soothing effect.
- One of the joys of colour is its practicability, a tool anyone can use inexpensively with little instruction and no danger — the use of a natural element in a practical way.
- Colour can be enormously helpful not only therapeutically, but also in such fields as meditation, tarot reading, distance healing, crystal-gazing, clairvoyance, mirror-gazing, etc.
- Each colour radiates its own particular vibration to which we respond.
- Symbolising season, direction, rank and royalty, colour is a vital healing force.
- The colours of a rainbow comprise energy vibrating at seven different frequencies which correspond to particular energy centres in our bodies, called chakras.
- A single ray of sunshine encompasses all the colours of the spectrum, yet the individual colours that we

see depend on which of the sun's rays are absorbed by the environment and which are reflected. For e.g. a leaf of a tree absorbs all the rays except for green, which is reflected and so we are able to see the leaf as green.

- Colour is everything, for colour is all what we are made of.

The Chakras

- There are seven principal chakras (or centres) which are essentially etheric, yet they coincide with various glands and colours in the physical body.

Chakra	Gland	Colours
Root	Perineum	Red
Sacral	Suprarenal	Orange
Solar Plexus	Lymph	Yellow
Heart	Thymus	Green
Throat	Thyroid	Blue
Third Eye	Pineal	Violet
Crown	Pituitary	White

- Each chakra has its own governing colour, and the seven colours of the chakras correspond to those of the spectrum.
- Each chakra in the body is an active centre of energy that expands to the surface of the body, thus connecting to the aura.
- Apart from the seven major chakras inside the body, there are three outside the physical body — the silver chakra located below our feet, the gold chakra, above our heads, and the black below the silver.

- There are also various secondary chakras in the joints of feet, ankles, knees, hips, shoulders, neck and hands.
- Energy moves into the chakras and out into the aura.
- Each chakra also has its emotional or spiritual aspect as well.
- Each chakra is also linked to specific life issues.
- In childhood, it is the root chakra at the base of the spine which strongly affects us, and later in life, the crown chakra influences us more.
- Our behaviour, attitude, our point of view all are affected by each chakra.
- Each chakra is influenced by the other, and does not act independently.
- We experience a feeling of abundance and well-being when the energy generated by the seven chakras is strong, and when it is weak, we experience sickness and frailty.
- Colour energy helps in realigning the chakras by its vibrational remedies.
- The silver or the eighth chakra, a secondary one, has its energy originating in the earth and drawn through the feet and upward, swirling around the uterus, breasts and tonsils.

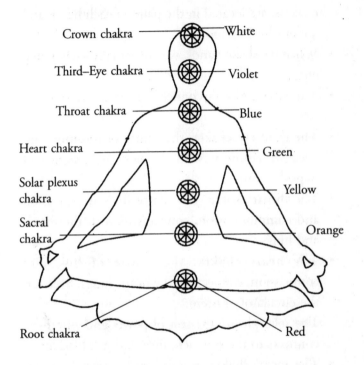

Crown chakra — White
Third–Eye chakra — Violet
Throat chakra — Blue
Heart chakra — Green
Solar plexus chakra — Yellow
Sacral chakra — Orange
Root chakra — Red

- The gold or the ninth chakra moves from over our heads down through the throat, heart, solar plexus, and genitals.
- The black or the twelfth chakra (the third external chakra of importance) constantly pushes us forward helping us in displacing stale energy.

11

- The tenth and eleventh chakras, called transmitter chakras, are located in the palm of each hand, and are our healing tools.
- When we shake hands, we are actually exchanging energy.
- The crown chakra connects us with the spiritual self.
- The third-eye chakra, the centre of intuition and wisdom, connects with the nervous system and hypothalamus.
- The throat chakra, the centre for self-expression and communication, connects us with the throat and lungs.
- The heart chakra, the centre of love and compassion, connects to the heart, lungs, liver and the circulatory system.
- The solar plexus, the seat of power and emotions, connects to the stomach, liver and gall bladder.
- The sacral chakra, the centre for sexual energy, feelings and emotions, connects with the gonads, testicles and ovaries.
- The root chakra, the seat of Kundalini energy, connects with the base of the spine and the suprarenal glands.

The Auras

- Human beings have their own energy field or aura, emitting electromagnetic waves.
- The auras that surround us are fields of colour.
- Our aura projects outwards from our bodies, usually measuring about 6 to 12 inches, though the distance can be greater.
- Auras, like finger prints, are unique to each individual, and are influenced by other auric fields.
- The size and brightness of the aura indicates our physical, mental, emotional and spiritual health at any given moment.
- Drugs, alcohol, negative traits, poor diet and stress weaken the auric field.
- Sunshine, meditation, regular exercises, being with nature, vibrational remedies and a positive attitude strengthen the auric field.
- To measure your auric field, rub your hands together vigorously; 7extend your arms sideways, palms facing each other; slowly bring your hands toward each other until you feel a slight resistance between them; the distance between the centre point and any one palm shows how far your aura extends from your body.

- To energise your life force, by massaging the aura, stand with hands loose by your sides; focus on a fixed point in front of you; begin spinning around clockwise, at least a minimum eleven times, though no more than twenty-one, but after each spin, bring your focus back to the fixed spot; stop and lie down; you will continue to feel the spinning sensations — this is good and as you go deeper, you will feel the energy surging in your life force.
- For the nervous system, the auric colours used during concentration are violet and lavender for soothing effects; grass green for relaxing effects; and yellow and orange for inspiring effects.
- For the organs of the body and the blood, clear dark blues are soothing; grass greens are ingrating; and bright reds are stimulating.
- Think of blue when you have a fever, high blood pressure, or hysteria.
- Thinking of red will ease cases of chill and restore the waning bodily warmth.

Colour Card Reading

- Colour cards and pendulums help us in finding out which chakra is out of balance, which colours we lack, or which we have excess of.
- Take seven cards and colour them red, orange, yellow, green, blue, purple, keeping the last one white.
- You can laminate them for durability after writing down the meaning of each chakra on the back of it.
- Jumble up the cards and lay them out in front of you in a row or two rows.
- Close your eyes and rub your palms together for a few minutes till you feel the warmth in your hands.
- Take a couple of deep breaths; then using any one of your palm, move your hand over the cards, about two inches high.
- Take your time moving your hand slowly over the cards, concentrating on the movement of your hand.
- When you begin to feel a pull, or a slightly heavy or hot feeling, hold your hand over the card which is drawing your hand.

- Open your eyes and check the card(s) chosen, and note the chakra that the card denotes — this is your main life process.
- When you have your hand being drawn to two cards, the one which has a stronger pull is the colour you need, the other is secondary.
- It is imperative to trust your gut feeling or inner wisdom which has led you to the card you were drawn to.
- While considering your colour needs, try to assess your present situation and see how you can utilise the colour energy till you feel right.

Red
Root Chakra—The Seat of Kundalini Power
This is the centre associated with survival issues and tribal connections. When drawn to this colour, you need to reconsider your relationship with your family and community, and overcome your fear of the future and death – depend on this red energy to give you succour and strength.

Orange
Sacral Chakra — The Emotions
This centre governs your emotions, relationships, and creativity. Being drawn to this colour involves a power

struggle associated with money and/or sex. Use this colour energy for help in guidance as regards desire, and express your creativity and life force.

Yellow
Solar Plexus Chakra — The Intellect
This is the centre of intuition, governing self-esteem. If drawn to this colour, find out where your inner power is being drained. Use this colour energy to develop your aptitude to make right decisions and to trust yourself.

Green
Heart Chakra — Love
This is the centre of unconditional love and compassion. If drawn to this colour, you probably need to rebase and let go of your anger, resentment, hurt, grief, etc, and also to repress being judgmental. Use this energy to encourage both self-love and trust, and to be forgiving.

Blue
Throat Chakra — Communication
This is the seat for communicating effectively and truthfully. If you require more blue, you may be deluding yourself in some way. Use this energy to invigorate your true individuality, will-power, and your power to convert dreams into realities.

Violet

Third-Eye Chakra — Intuition

This is the centre of intuition that helps you to view life objectively. It also connects you to your spiritual self. When drawn to this colour energy, it is time to connect with your Self, and contemplate on the people and situations in your life.

White

Crown Chakra — The Divine

This is your spiritual self. When drawn to this colour, it is time for you to reconnect with the higher consciousness and to help others. Since white is the symbol of purity, allow this energy to cleanse your being of negative and blocked energies.

Using a Pendulum

- A pendulum can also be used to verify which colour energy you need.
- Write the names of the seven colours of a spectrum, an inch apart, on a piece of paper.
- Take a few deep breaths.
- Dangle the pendulum from your hand over the tip of the word or colour, holding it a few inches over it.

- Ask the pendulum in which direction will be 'yes'.
- Though you are not moving the string of the pendulum, your unconscious self activates your muscles and nerves, causing the pendulum to swing either clockwise, counter-clockwise, back and forth, or side to side. Note the movement as 'yes'.
- Similarly, ask which direction will be 'no'.
- Now hold the pendulum over the word or colour on your paper, and determine the colour energy your body requires.

The Power of Colours

Red : Passion

- Red symbolises love and procreation, but it is also associated with violence and death.
- In general, it is most often related with our most primal instincts, procreation and aggression.
- The Chinese still traditionally wear red in the marriage ceremonies for good luck.
- For Christians, red symbolises the sacrificial blood of Christ, and the colour of vestments worn by cardinals, but is also associated with Hell and the Devil.
- While the red colour is associated with the planet Mars and zodiac sign Scorpio, the element is represented by fire.
- The crystal garnet, and the gemstone ruby typify the colour red.
- Red is associated with the root chakra, the first chakra, at the base of the spinal column, which is the energy centre.
- This energy centre gives us our fire power as it is associated with the element fire.

- This is where our survival instincts are located.
- It is the source of our strength, courage, leadership, energy and will.
- This energy centre is connected to the physical body and related to the male energy.
- This strong primal energy connects us all, being associated with belonging to parents, grandparents, and to other people.
- With the chakra perfectly balanced, you feel active and at home within yourself, among your family, in the society and the world.
- You feel strongly connected with your own body and with other people.
- You feel protected and confident that things will work out the right way for you.
- When this natural flow of energy is blocked, you feel detached, estranged from others, and belligerent.
- If something is not going right for you and is making you feel wretched, then you need to use some red energy.
- Working on the issues related to the root chakra can help everyone resolve family problems and also help the other chakras to function efficiently.

- Always make sure that no family beliefs are blocking your personal expression.
- Explore your fears regarding the future and/or death, and use the red energy to overcome these hurdles.
- If you have red in excess, you tend to be aggressive, egotistic, domineering, greedy, sexually indiscriminate and restless — to balance, use green followed by a small dose of red.
- If you lack the colour red, you lack confidence, feel weak and fearful of being abandoned, are self-destructive, and rely on outside belief systems to support your actions — therefore, you need more of red.
- You feel focused, grounded, healthy, abundant and energetic when you have had just enough red.

Visualisation
- Remove the shade from a table lamp, and fix a red bulb.
- Sit in silence for a few minutes, breathing deeply.
- See yourself enveloped in red.
- Within this red light, you are balanced, strong, courageous, and safe.

- Visualise yourself filled with energy and happiness.
- You are safe and relaxed in your body.
- Take a deep breath and believe in this image of relaxation and safety.

Grounding Meditation
- Close your eyes and breathe deeply and slowly for a few minutes.
- Imagine a cord, like a tail, emanating from the base of your spine.
- Visualise this cord effortlessly melting through matter as it gets longer and longer; melting through the chair you are seated upon, then the floor, then the various levels of the building your are in, going deeper and deeper into the earth.
- Imagine a large crystal in the centre of the earth.
- Visualise your cord coiling around this crystal three times, and then secure it with a knot.
- Sit in silence for a while and experience what it feels like to be grounded to the earth.
- Now allow the red energy from the earth move up your cord into your pelvic area.
- Feel the assurance of this warm grounding energy at the base of your spine radiating out to your hips.
- Sit with this energy till you feel completely grounded and secure.

Orange : The Emotions

- Buddhists have always associated orange as a symbol of wisdom, intuition, spontaneity, and living in the present moment.
- The Chinese and Japanese consider this colour as a sign of joy and happiness.
- The second chakra, the sacral chakra, is based in the centre of abdomen, above the root chakra and below the solar plexus chakra (which is yellow).
- Since orange is a combination of red and yellow, hence this chakra shares some of the traits of its neighbours — the root chakra (red) and the solar plexus chakra (yellow).
- It controls sexual desires, instincts, feelings and creativity.
- It is the centre of our power, emotions and intuition.
- The orange chakra energy lets us progress beyond the security and limitation of the tribe, and form relationships outside our families.
- We receive emotional guidance in the form of gut feeling from this chakra.
- We must listen to our instincts, and when we don't like what we hear, we must realise that it is an area we need to work on.

- Orange is associated with the planet moon, the element water, the crystal carnelian, and the gemstone pearl.
- The orange chakra being our pleasure centre, we register the sensations of touch, smell, sound, sight and taste.
- When the chakra is in perfect balance, we feel excitement and zestful about life, we relish and enjoy, express our creativity and sexuality.
- All these positive vibrations attract others towards us.
- This, in turn, is socially vitalising, and we feel an easy connection with those around us.
- When there is imbalance in the chakra, we tend to have problems with ethics, sexuality, honour and money.
- This chakra is also where laughter originates, and in balance, allows us to establish positive relations not only with our mates and lovers, but also with other people around us.
- This orange energy centre gives us the power to embody all that we desire.
- During childhood, when our chakras are sensitive, we pick up the obscurest of energies, especially those connected to our creativity and sexuality.

- When our families encourage our spirit of inventiveness and spontaneity, and accept and endorse sensuality, we experience a sense of freedom with our naked bodies, free of inhibitions.
- When negative parental attitudes, leading to sexual blockage, get passed on from generation to generation, there is a dire need to visit the orange chakra to rejuvenate oneself.
- People feel guilt-ridden about sexual desire and diffident at work when they have an underactive orange chakra.
- An excess of orange can cause people to be sexually indiscriminate whereby they use sexual energy to manipulate others, and get angry very quickly if rebuffed.
- Too much orange can leave you aggressive, overindulgent, overambitious, emotionally explosive, manipulative, obsessed with sex, seeing people as sex objects, and prone to hyperactivity — use blue followed by a small amount of orange to balance your chakra.
- Too little orange will have you feeling resentful, sensitive, distrustful, harbouring feelings of guilt and sexual repressions, and not being open about your feelings.

- A perfectly balanced orange chakra makes you friendly, caring, creative, intuitive, optimistic and connected to your feelings.
- Always remember that as enlightened beings our intuition will always guide us to the right choices.

Visualisation
- Sit in silence in a quiet room for a few minutes.
- Take a few deep and long breaths, and see yourself engulfed in a beautiful orange light.
- You are connected to your inner wisdom which guides all your emotions and actions.
- You are competent enough to resolve all situations effectively.
- You are gratified with power and sexuality.
- Breathe this in.

Meditation
- Fix an orange bulb in a table lamp and leave the shade on.
- Set quietly and absorb the orange light for a while.
- Depending upon your body's need, you will feel either relaxed or stimulated.
- Allow creativity to flow into you from the chakra.

- Affirm to yourself that you are receptive to a deep inner wisdom.
- Ponder over how you deal with people closest to you.
- Affirm your wish to be good to others and that all your relationships bring joy to you.
- Allow this orange energy to mitigate your need to control situations.
- Trust that your inner wisdom will always be there for guidance.

Yellow : The Intellect

- The colour changes its qualities according to its tint : the warmer its tone, the more positive the connections, the more it is tinged with green, the more negative it becomes.
- Yellow and gold have been associated with the divine symbols of creation since time immemorial.
- The Chinese consider yellow as a sacred colour symbolising the centre of the earth.
- In heraldry, gold is an emblem of love, wisdom and loyalty.
- In general parlance, yellow is associated with cowardice.

- The yellow chakra, the solar plexus which is the third chakra, is the seat of the intellect end personal power.
- It is associated with the planet sun, the zodiac sign Leo, the element air, the crystal heliodor, and the gemstone topaz.
- The solar plexus chakra, located between the rib cage and the navel, is related to the adrenal glands.
- This energy centre, our command centre, allows us to advance towards fulfilment of our desires and goals, as this is the site where our thoughts and opinions are formed.
- The yellow energy activates our thought process, enabling us to exercise our intellect that we need to make decisions and move ahead.
- It also stimulates us into taking risks for developing close relationships with others.
- After the orange chakra, this is our second intuitive centre which we need to develop fully, to fortify our intellectual decisions and steer our course in life.
- The yellow energy emanating from the solar plexus chakra bolsters our inner power and helps our self-esteem to grow and flourish.

- You are drawn to the yellow energy when you need to have more trust in yourself and in your instincts, which gives you an amazing sense of power and confidence.
- Consciously do things while dealing with issues of self-esteem, as this will help you have a better opinion of yourself.
- You need to assess people and situations in your life responsible for draining you of positive energy, and take action accordingly.
- Too much of yellow is likely to make you a workaholic, a perfectionist, judgmental, demanding, sexually unfulfilled, and an egotist — balance it with violet or purple followed by a small dose of yellow.
- A dearth of yellow energy will leave you depressed, insecure, afraid of being alone, jealous and suspicious in love relationships, worried about what others think, weighed down by a low opinion of yourself, and seeking other's approval.
- A perfectly balanced yellow chakra will make you intelligent, charismatic, respectful, happy, relaxed, expressive and expansive, strengthened by a strong feeling of personal power.

Visualisation

- For at least a week, go to bed earlier than usual.
- Breathe deeply and focus your attention on your solar plexus.
- Imagine yourself cocooned in this warm light emanating from the energy chakra.
- In this sunshine filled space, picture yourself as a child playing.
- Introduce yourself to this child and nurture it as though it were your own.
- Talk to her/him, complementing how beautiful, intelligent and clever she/he is.
- Continue to hold this visual till you fall asleep — this will expose your subconsciousness to healing.
- It is said that when we go to sleep whatever it is that we are thinking about is what our deep subconscious meditates on while we sleep — so always go to sleep with good, positive thoughts.
- Continue nurturing your child for the rest of the week, and you will feel the positive change in your self-esteem instantly.

Green : The Heart

- Since ancient days, green has been symbolised as the soul's regeneration.
- Some even associate it with jealousy and envy ("green with envy", "green-eyed monster").
- Muslims associate green as the colour of the prophet Mohammed, who is believed to have been protected by angels in green turbans.
- Christians believe green to be the colour of contemplation, being equidistant from the blue of heaven and the red of hell.
- They also consider green as a symbol of hope, as borne out by Christ's cross and the Holy Grail portrayed as green.
- The Chinese consider the green jade as a lucky stone.
- The heart chakra, the fourth chakra, is the green energy chakra located in the centre of the chest near the heart, and related to the thymus.
- This energy chakra is the seat of love, compassion, kindness and tolerance.
- It connects the three physical chakras of the lower body to the three spiritual chakras in the upper body, uniting matter and spirit.

- This is also the centre where our male and female energies meet.
- The green energy chakra is associated with the planet Venus, the zodiac signs Taurus and Libra, the element air, the crystal green tourmaline, and the gemstone emerald.
- When the heart chakra is well balanced, we feel loved, safe, open to be loved, take risks and are able to trust.
- We are able to forgive others despite their faults.
- More importantly, we are able to give ourselves too unconditional love that we always hunger for.
- As we start loving ourselves, we release the negative energy that is trapped inside.
- A balanced heart chakra enables you to feel connected with everybody, shaking off feelings of loneliness.
- We are able to purge ourselves of a tendency to be judgmental, and of being critical of others.
- Excess of green can make you demanding, judgmental, possessive, melodramatic, oversensitive and vulnerable to getting embroiled in emotional blackmail — balance by using green, followed by pink or soft reds.

- Too little green will make you feel unworthy of love, frightened of rejection, sorry for yourself, unforgiving and suspicious, indecisive and paranoid.
- The right amount of green ensures that you are friendly, forgiving, compassionate, empathic, in touch with your feelings, and one who sees the world with love.
- There is a possibility that you are drawn to a green card because you are probably holding on to grief and/or anger, some resentment which needs to be released to make you positive and forgiving, as forgiveness clears your energy system.
- When we don't forgive, we carry on surrendering power to the person who did us wrong, which affects our ability to love and be loved and our physical well-being — "think green" and release your negative energy.
- Green colour also has the power to calm down the nervous system.

Visualisation
- Sit in silence for a few minutes.
- Imagine your heart region glowing in the green tint that seems ideal to you.

- See this glow spreading as you take in deep breaths.
- You are loosening your hold on your anger, grief and pain.
- You are being permeated with pure love energy.
- This love energy stretches outward, as far outward as your mind can visualise, into the infinite universe.
- Feel the love energy flowing out and feel the abundant love energy flowing in.
- Breathe this in.

Blue : Communication

- All Hindus, Buddhists, native Americans and Chinese associate blue with the heavens.
- Christians use the colour to epitomise Virgin Mary.
- The ancient Romans associated it with Zeus and Venus.
- According to Hindu Mythology, Krishna is coloured blue, as is Vishnu.
- In many primitive civilisations, people wore blue stones as amulets to ward off evil.
- The throat chakra, the fifth centre of energy with its blue electromagnetic vibrations, is the centre of communication, self-expression, knowledge and wisdom.

- This is the centre where we find our higher potential and absorb our dreams.
- With a well-balanced throat chakra, we are able to communicate honestly and with love.
- This energy chakra is associated with the planet Jupiter, the zodiac signs Gemini and Virgo, the element ether, the gemstone sapphire and the crystal aquamarine.
- This chakra is considered in ancient Hindu texts as the purification chakra where the divine nectar of infinity dwells, and the thyroid gland here can be stimulated through yogic practice.
- When there is a blockage in this chakra, you feel you are compromising yourself, you have something to say to some person but are unable to do so, you are incapable of communicating effectively — these manifest as a physical problem in your throat, or you get into a depression.
- The blue energy centre reinforces your connection to divine intelligence.
- It stimulates your true personality, and helps to ensure that you make the right decisions and stick to them.

- The blue throat chakra, like the yellow and orange, helps us experience greater abundance in our lives by endowing us with greater strength of will and passion to turn dreams into realities.
- With excessive blue energy, you may become arrogant, addictive, self-righteous, too garrulous, talking before you think, and uncompromising — balance this chakra by using orange followed by a small amount of blue.
- When the blue energy is deficient, you tend to be timid and quiet, inconsistent, undependable, devious, lacking self-control and communicative ability, and likely to compromise too effortlessly.
- The right amount of blue will have you focused, living in the present, and being able to live and speak your truth, be a good speaker, and also be artistic.
- A secondary chakra between the heart and the throat is linked to aqua which is a mixture of blue and green; this colour has a strong effect on our immune system.

Visualisation

- Sit silently and breathe in and out slowly and deeply.
- Visualise yourself or the area you want to remedy engulfed by a blue light.
- Visualise yourself handling the situation fruitfully in resolving the issues.
- Realise that your intentions come from love.
- Breathe this image in.

Violet : The Spirit

- According to Christian tradition, purple robes represented repentance, penance, sermon and Christ's blood.
- Today, Christians associate purple with the advent of Easter.
- A large section of the world today believes that over the next decade or so, our consciousness will evolve into the third-eye or violet chakra, bringing in an era of peace, harmony and community consciousness.
- The third-eye chakra, the sixth chakra, emits violet/purple energy.
- This chakra is located between the eyebrows, and is connected to the pituitary gland.
- This is the seat where we connect to our self.

- This energy centre allows us to be intuitive, as it is the seat of knowledge and understanding.
- It moderates the energies between the physical and the spiritual.
- It empowers us to stimulate our psychic powers and turn our dreams into reality.
- This energy centre is associated with zodiac sign Libra, the element telepathic energy, the crystal amethyst, and the gemstone purple ruby.
- The energy from this centre helps to balance the left (rational) and right (intuitive) halves of the brain.
- It is also believed that this is the centre that helps us reflect back to our past experiences.
- Intuition, wisdom and detachment allow this chakra to open the passage between our conscious and our unconscious self.
- The centre reveals to us how everything we undergo or experience has a symbolic meaning and direction.
- Excessive violet may make you manipulative, authoritative and a religious fanatic, an egotist who goes around with the head in the clouds — balance by using yellow followed by a small amount of violet.

- An overactive violet chakra also makes you hypersensitive and impatient, worrying a lot.
- An underactive third-eye chakra makes you undisciplined, highly sensitive, wary of success, oblivious of what is going on around you, superstitious, forgetful and fearful of death.
- The right amount of violet will have you connected to the self, the infinite wisdom and the cosmic consciousness; you will be charismatic, unattached to material objects, and unafraid of death.
- There is every reason now to believe that our psychic abilities are beginning to expand and that we are getting connected to our higher self, looking at people and situations in life objectively.
- We have the potential in this energy centre to merge our powers of reason with divine wisdom.
- With the wisdom, knowledge and trust of the third eye, we realise that there is no separation even in death, that we must let go and move on.

Visualisation
- Sitting in a quiet room, take deep breaths for a few minutes.
- Visualise your third-eye chakra glowing with violet light and connecting you to your self.

- You are relaxed, calm and receptive to all information.
- You can discern truth without being judgmental.
- You can see people and situations as they are, without dread or longing.
- You are letting your intuitive wisdom to relay messages to your conscious mind.
- Breathe this in.

White : The Divine

- For aeons, white has been associated with purity by many cultures.
- For Hindus, white is the symbol of self-illumination.
- The Christians consider white to denote purity, sainthood and the Holy Spirit.
- The white wedding dress worn in Christian marriages symbolises a virginal state as well as the bride leaving the old behind and moving into the new.
- According to Chinese tradition, white symbolises virginity, purity, age, autumn and also misfortune!
- In many cultures, white garments are used as priestly vestments.

- The crown chakra is the seventh chakra which has white electromagnetic waves.
- This energy chakra, located at the top of the head, is the centre of our spiritual life.
- With this chakra open, we are one with the universal life force.
- This energy centre is connected with the pineal gland, and is believed to have a strong influence over the aging process.
- This white chakra, which unites us with our source, is known as the *sahasrara* chakra, or the thousand-petaled lotus, the one thousand representing infinity, and hence the connection with our source.
- According to the Vedic texts, white light is symbolic of nirvana, the ultimate state of being.
- Like the Christians, the Hindus too associate white with God and the divine spirit.
- The Vedic texts proclaim that we, like the rainbow, are made of a white light source which is divine.
- This White energy chakra is associated with the planet Moon, the zodiac sign Cancer, the element cosmic energy, the crystal clear quartz, and the gemstone diamond.

- We experience a feeling of oneness with the Infinite when our white energy chakra is perfectly balanced.
- We then enjoy an understanding of our continuously evolving spiritual essence.
- It allows to us to experience our connection with all sentient beings, which makes us compassionate and helpful to them.
- An excessive amount of white energy may leave you depressed, destructive, easily frustrated, and unable to use your full potential — balance by adding red followed by a small amount of white.
- You also feel alienated and confused as you lack inspiration.
- A scant amount of white may also leave you depressed as well as make you indecisive as you live in conflict with your spiritual beliefs.
- A perfectly balanced white chakra allows you to be open to the divine, be able to live according to your spiritual beliefs, and transcend all things material and mundane, and be positive with all negative blocks removed.
- Since white has a strong cleansing vibration, it is particularly effective in wiping out negativity in us.

- When you are drawn to white, it could mean that it is time for you to reconnect with your origin and your spirituality.
- It could mean that some negativity is blocking your energy from connecting you to the divine, and you need to work upon it.
- It is a sign for you to book at life, and see if you are living in accordance with your spiritual beliefs, if you are open-minded about the spiritual beliefs of others, and if you are asking more than you give.
- The white energy allows you to move into your tranquil space, and see the rejoicing of you and your relationship with the universe.

Colour Energy Exercises

- Find out which colour(s) will be most instrumental in balancing your energy centres by using the colour card reading method or the pendulum.
- Once this is done, you can absorb the colour energy using any of the following exercises.
- Try them all out, and find out which ones appeal to you most and are most effective.
- The following easy-to-do exercises will help you, with daily practice, to find yourself increasingly aware of their effects.
- Before you commence your exercises, prepare yourself with some deep rhythmic breathing. That will help your body to be receptive to colour energies.

Deep Rhythmic Breathing
- You may stand, or be seated, keeping your spine straight and head erect.
- While breathing in, imagine yourself being filled with your breath.
- Feel the air passing through your nose, down your spine, and up again to fill your chest.

- Place your right hand above your navel and your left hand on your chest to get used to this movement.
- Gently releasing the breath, feel it going down your chest.
- Feel your chest and stomach deflating.
- Feel the heaviness of the breath being exhaled out, carrying with it toxins and carbon dioxide.
- Feel the air exiting from the lower portion of your nose.
- See that your tongue is relaxed, your jaw loose and lips together.
- Before starting the next inhalation, pause for a few seconds, when you feel that time does not exist and that you are fully in the present moment, your awareness increases.
- Your breath becomes rhythmic and continuous.
- As you visualise your breath, allowing thoughts to fleet-by like passing clouds, feel the negativity and tension draining from you.
- The deep, focused breathing helps in converting the air we breathe-in into positive energy.
- All the thoughts that pass by during breathing, affect the vibrancy of the energy, but trust yourself of doing it the right way, and you will do so.

- To get the rhythm going, practise it in silence, and then use it in your everyday life to relieve tension and fear.

Colour Shower
- The colour shower is extremely beneficial in balancing your chakras. For e.g. if you are worried or feeling tense, a blue shower will calm you down.
- Check and decide what colour you require.
- Start off with the rhythmic deep breathing exercise.
- Visualise the perfect shade of your colour.
- Imagine it sprinkling down from the universe into your crown chakra, down through your body, down each arm, each leg, and exiting through your feet. ·
- The wisdom of the colour energy allows it to go wherever it is needed in the body, and removes all the negative blocks while doing so, making you feel exhilarated and refreshed.
- The whole process takes about less than two minutes.

White Bubble Protection
- White being a protective energy, this particular exercise is best during times when you feel negative vibes from others, or when you are in a difficult or grim situation.

- Start with the deep breathing rhythm.
- Imagine that you are enveloped by a huge white energy bubble that stretches six to twelves inches from your body.
- Feel yourself being drained of and sheltered from any other negative energy around you.
- You can also visualise such a bubble around another person, situation or place that has negative energy which needs to be cleared.

  For e.g. when you feel apprehensive about an operation, visualise a white bubble surrounding you, and this stays till the task is done, making you feel safe and relaxed.
- Another technique is to visualise what you want (to be elected as the president a bank, for example), and dispatch it into the universe in a bubble — it may work!

Colour Sunbath

- A simple and joyful way to absorb colour energy is through coloured glass.
- You can make a 36-inch square using coloured cellophane.
- This exercise should be done on a sunny day.
- Determine what colour you need to balance.

- Using a tape, fix the coloured cellophane on the lower half of a sunny window.
- Sit in front of the window, allowing the sun to stream in through the cellophane onto your body.
- Breathe deeply for ten minutes or so.
- Many colour therapists use this technique to heal physical conditions.

Spinning Chakras

- With this exercise, all the chakras can be balanced, or even each chakra can be brought individually into balance.
- Commence with the deep breathing rhythmic exercise.
- Lie down and dangle a pendulum above your body.
- Check one chakra at a time, beginning with the red chakra.
- If you see the pendulum not spinning clockwise, keep holding it steady, and soon it will stop and reverse the spinning direction.
- Once all the chakras are well balanced, lay aside the pendulum.
- Visualise the colour of the chakra that you need to work on.
- Imagine the chakra spinning three times to the right, and then three times to left.

- To rebalance all your chakras, begin with red and finish with white.
- Apart from balancing your chakras, you will also be balancing your male-female energies.

Coloured Fabric Swatches
- Place a swatch of coloured cotton cloth over the chakra which needs to be balanced.
- Do the deep breathing exercise.
- Lie down and place the fabric over the chakra you need to work on, or you can place it over each of the seven chakras in case you want to balance all of them.
- Breathe deeply into the fabric-covered areas.
- Mentally declare to yourself that you are balancing your energy system.
- Do this for as long as you can, good if you can do it for five minutes.

Solarising Water
- Water can be beneficial if energised by one of the colour frequencies.
- Select the chakra that needs to be balanced, and its corresponding colour will come into play.
- Take a transparent glass or plastic container of the colour that you need.

- Fill it with water and keep it in the sun for maximum time.
- The water will be energised with the vibrations of the colour.
- Sip it slowly to get maximum benefit.
- Store it in the refrigerator for a few days — water of the warmer colours of the lower three chakras cannot be stored for too long, while waters of the cooler colours of the top three or four chakras can be kept a little longer.
- You can fill water into seven glasses of different colours, and solarise them all together, one for each of the different chakras — water from each glass has a distinctly different taste.
- In case you don't have a coloured glass or plastic container, you can wrap any transparent container with a transparent piece of silk or any other light fabric of the colour of the chakra you wish to work on.

Colour Meditation
- Colour meditation is a simple and effective application.
- Visualise each of the chakra colours in turn to see which colour you need the most — one or two will vibrate.

- Have faith in your inner wisdom to guide you to the right colour(s).
- Take a few deep breaths.
- As you inhale, imagine the colour enveloping you completely.
- As you exhale, imagine the colour showering down into the top of your body, flowing through your body, and out through the feet, suffusing your whole body with the colour.
- Imagine the colour taking a particular form and dancing — for each person, the experience will be different, so enjoy it as you see and feel it.
- You can complete your meditation with another colour if you so desire.
- To cleanse your body of all negativity, and for general purification, meditate on white.
- Use green meditation to heal internal organs and for hurt emotions.
- To cleanse your aura, use the colour pink while meditating.
- Meditate on blue colour to calm yourself.
- The ideal time for the colour meditation would be in the morning and before going to bed.
- Five to fifteen minutes of colour meditation would be beneficial.

Projecting Colour

- This technique is specifically used for healing particular areas of the body.
- This exercise is mainly directed to healing another person, though you can use this on yourself too.
- When you master this technique, you can even go for long-distance healing.
- Before you begin this exercise, it is essential that you ground and balance yourself (see page 23).
- Determine the colour that your friend requires.
- Seek permission from the person to help him heal.
- Tell your friend to do a few deep breathing rhythmic exercises.
- Stretch out your hand, that you commonly use, in front of you.
- Imagine your crown chakra opening up to the universe, and repeat to yourself, "I am open and receptive to the light and love of the universe."
- Visualise the perfect shade of the colour you are going to use, and ask the other person also to do likewise.
- Invoke the powers of the universe and request that the colour be conducted in your body through your head and out through your palms.

- Place your hand on the auric level of your friend's body that needs the energy.
- Visualise this colour energy flowing gently from you into the persons body, curing the illness and pain, and also energising the body.

Creative Art
- Painting and colouring are good ways of giving yourself colour energy, and removing any blockage that is within you.
- The best way of allowing art to be creative is by allowing yourself the freedom to do whatever you please and to let your hand create whatever is done on impulse, even if it happens to be just two strokes of colour.
- The important thing to remember is that style comes out of imperfection and striving to get an image down on paper.
- Do not have any fast or rigid notions about art as such, but give a free rein to your imagination and hand.
- You may soon realise that, though the artwork may look grotesque or meaningless, you feel a sense of relief and relaxation because all your negativity has

poured out in the form of art, thus cleansing your energy chakras.

- So allow the drawing or painting to take its own form and colour.

Balancing Male-Female Energy

- An imbalance between our male and female energies is the root cause for many of our ailments.
- This leads to our thoughts and actions being in disharmony.
- You may have many ideas which you are unable to convert into actions, and the reason may be because your male energy is not supporting its counterpart.
- You may find yourself being unnecessarily harsh with some people, and this may be due to lack of support by your female energy to your male energy.
- To balance both energies, first imagine a golden ray, the male energy, showering down through your head, down to your heart chakra, turning clockwise.
- Imagine a silver ray (the female energy) moving up through your feet to your heart chakra, and turning counter-clockwise.
- See them begin to merge together, and both your energies harmonising.

Colours of Love

- Love energy is the fuel of the heart chakra.
- We spend a lot of time thinking about and acting upon love.
- In an unconditional love, we are in harmony with our true nature and with the tide of the universe.
- When we love, we are happy, letting go of our fear.
- Love is the only reality, the only truth, the elixir that allows us to live in consonance with ourselves and our world.
- Love is the symbol of the Divine in us.

Loving Yourself

- You may love your family, friends, partner, or anybody else, but what is of primary concern is loving yourself.
- We need to love ourselves as we are and not as who we were, or want to be someday.
- We should learn to love ourselves as if we are unique, and not compare ourselves with others.
- We need to be glad to be ourselves, and recognise the love what God has endowed us with.

- People who believe in some way that they don't deserve love have developed negative emotional patterns to make them unhappy.
- When someone chooses not to be with you, probably this rejection is necessary for you to have time for self-reflection.
- We need positive and close contact with others to keep our energy flowing.
- By loving ourselves, treating ourselves with kindness and unconditional open-mindedness that we seek from others, we will attract the love we crave for.
- The ideal dream is to be in love, to merge yourself with another, but in such a case either one of you will lose your individual power, creating an energy imbalance.
- So, to lose yourself in your own self-love is something which will give you the same satisfaction as merging into another being.
- It is very assuring to know that you can fill yourself with the positive energy that your lover would have provided.
- Just remember that if you fall in love with yourself, so will others, so hold onto your power to love yourself unconditionally.

Colour Energising Yourself

- While green represents the heart chakra on the physical plane, pink symbolises it on the spiritual level.
- So envelope yourself with both green and pink to fortify your self-love.
- Treat yourself to a green or pink colour shower.
- Imagine yourself suffused in pink, floating peacefully in the universe.
- Add pink colouring agent to your bath water, and soak in it, caressing your body lovingly with your hands, absorbing the heating pink energy, for self-touch is healing.
- Start your own "I love myself" routine — meditate on this thought and visualise either green or deep pink colour which will create the vibration that increases your self-love as well as attracts other's love.
- You can send yourself healing energy from your future self to your present self, or from your past to your present — you start loving memories as if they are your children, and soon, within a day or two, you will find yourself filled with a wave of warmth.

Energising Colour for Finding Love

- Create a harmonising environment for yourself by surrounding yourself with lots of plants and flowers for fresh energy.
- Have a lot of blue colour around you to ease the sense of loneliness.
- Include a lot of green in your environment for self-love, and pink to attract attention.
- Your aim should be to achieve a state of self-sustaining happiness which will make you feel whole and complete on your own.
- Your essence, which is pure love and creativity, will make you fall in love with yourself.
- This focus on your personal growth and creativity will lead to a higher self-esteem and attracting a mate who is also full of positive energy.
- Surround yourself with green, wear green, and visualise green.
- Use pink which fuses perfectly primal passion and purity.
- Hold a pink quartz or malachite crystal during meditation to help cleanse your mind and heart.
- Keep this crystal with you all the time whose energy will attract, and help you focus on the kind of person you want to meet.

- Use a lot of pink — in makeup, pink flowers in your bedroom, pink candle, pink clothes — it always gives a fresh, youthful look and glow connected with new love.
- Use a lot of red too — red undergarments, red nails and lips, red ornaments, red flowers — red stimulates passion and sexual energy.
- Use orange to connect you to your intuition, especially in matters related to the heart and love.
- Use purple, wear purple, bathe in purple, meditate on purple so that your third-eye chakra binds you to your higher self to determine whether your new love mate is right for you.
- Remember that a yellow candle brings joy, whether you love someone or not.

Finding the Perfect Mate

- List all the qualities that you would like to see in your ideal partner — compassion, generosity, sense of humour, etc.
- Check this list and honestly ask yourself what are the qualities listed that are in you.
- The few that you don't possess are the qualities you need to develop in yourself.
- When you attempt to become what you seek, you will meet your match.

Loving a Partner

- A relationship with a loving partner creates a true energetic exchange.
- An energetic bond connects the partners at the solar plexus, and the stronger the tie, the stronger the cord which binds them together.
- In healthy relationships, the energy exchange is reciprocal, but when the energy is not returned, the person holding on feels drained, while the other person feels invaded.
- Keep your solar plexus, the yellow energy centre, balanced so that your relationship with your partner is strong.
- Yellow helps in maintaining your self-esteem and confidence which, in turn, helps you to have reciprocal energy exchange.
- If either of you feels insecure, you need to treat yourselves to the yellow energy and also green energy to make sure that you have no resentment towards each other.
- Cocoon yourself in blue once in a while to ensure that you are having on honest and effective communication.
- Married couples should make sure that their environment includes green for love, orange for

sexuality, blue for honest communication, white for cleansing, and black for progress and a healthy relationship.

- If you have arguments with your partners, use white to clear away mental blocks and negativity built up between you.
- In case you need to make decisions that involve your partner, use violet.
- For mending love, use pink to restore the feeling of newness and create a healing atmosphere.
- Red and white carnations in your bedroom will absorb any negativity that is in the room.
- By wearing and visualising orange, you will know whether mending your relationship with your partner is truly ideal.
- Wearing blue and sleeping on blue sheets lets you both speak the truth, which, though can be painful, may help you learn much from it.
- When love is strained, using purple pillowcases stimulates dreams which can help reveal the truth about your relationship.
- Wear white, use white, visualise white, use the white bubble meditation to cleanse any past or present negativity.

Love and Sex

- Red and orange chakras are the energetic centres of our sensual world.
- Many highly evolved people have used the sexual energy for reaching higher states of consciousness.
- Besides using red for primal passion and procreation, and orange for sexuality and desire, some people use other colours also to get in the mood to make love.
- Each individual has to work out for himself which colour will stimulate and enhance his sexual feelings and responses.
- For some women, it is green or pink that enhances their passion.
- For people beset with a feeling of spiritual communion, purple or white is the ideal choice.
- At the moment of orgasm, some people see various colours which generally reveal something about the other person and his/her relationship.

Loving Friends

- Female friendship is particularly filled with healing love energy.
- When families and friends intentionally create a loving environment for each other, their energy

radiates to the broader community, which in turn helps to positively energise the world around.

- Hence it is necessary for all of us to have our daily energy exchanges, and be conscious of the energy we give out — all our actions should show love.

Gift of Colour Energy

- When you buy gifts for someone, consider what colour he or she might need.
- For an ailing person, something in red, white or yellow would energise the immune system and lift up his spirits.
- A wedding gift can be silver for stability, green for unconditional love, white for moving forward, blue for honesty, and red for passion.
- For a newborn baby, something in green for unconditional love would be wonderful.
- An engagement gift can be of the colour red or orange for passion and purple or white for a strong emotional bond.
- For a broken-hearted friend, something in pink will fill the void with a sense of self, or green for self-love.
- For a funeral, violet or purple flowers or wreaths will help one to connect to the spirit of the person who has passed away.

Colours of Success

- The universe is a place of limitless abundance, and it offers success to all of us.
- In order to be well grounded, confident and at ease, success requires that your energy flow through you freely.
- The two chakras associated with success are the throat and root chakras.
- Red, the root chakra, connotes assertiveness, while blue, the throat chakra, signifies effective communication, both important for success in life.
- You need to communicate in ways that people understand.
- You will enjoy health, happiness and success once you understand your energy system.
- You will start trusting your instinct and will not be afraid of making major decisions or changing your mind, because you will realise what your intuition is telling you to do.
- You will be open to accept the messages from your higher self, and you will find success in what you seek.

If on the Wrong Career Path

- If you feel frustrated, unhappy, and hate the thought of going to work at all, the first thing you need to do is cleanse yourself with white — wear white; sleep on white sheets, for during sleep, our system is more receptive to assimilating energy; and have a white colour shower.

- Take an orange colour shower, and wear orange to strengthen your intuition, for orange energy fills you with the power to take action and move on.

- Yellow increases your self-esteem and inner power, and will help you to take action.

Finding the Right Career Path

- A clear energy field will attract people who are in a position to help you with a higher level of work.

- Be receptive to all possibilities.

- Even if the job is not what you were seeking, notice how you feel when you think and talk about it, for the right path may not be the one you had in mind.

- Give yourself an orange shower, and wear orange for intuition.

- View a yellow painting to help stimulate your intellect.

- Hold a green malachite or calcite crystal to clear your cluttered mind, and be receptive to receive messages from your heart about what path to follow.

- When you take an energy shower with purple, you get connected to your higher self, and you will always be guided the right way.
- The purple energy, while promoting objectivity and protecting you from hassles of money worries and preconceived notions, allows you to properly see things in their correct perspective, making way for clarity.

Finding Work

- While looking for a job or pondering over the course of action to be taken, notice how you feel.
- Use the pink bubble technique to launch your ambitions into the universe.
- While visualising yourself in your ideal job, meditate on gold and purple as they both help to transform thoughts into action.
- Allow these two colours to engulf you while you think of the perfect job, giving you the power to shine.
- Use white to cleanse yourself to prevent any subconscious negativity in blocking your energy.

Handling the Interview

- You need to wear red undergarments for courage and assertiveness.

- Avoid wearing red or bright pink dresses or shirts for they are too aggressive and may have adverse effects.
- A blue scarf or tie round the throat activates the chakra whose energy helps in effective communication and in instilling personal integrity.
- Wear orange somewhere on your person for enhanced intuition.
- Burn an orange candle in your work area or at home the night before to aid in your positive communication.
- Have an orange and yellow energy shower before the interview to enhance your intuition and stimulate your intellect to assess the situation and act accordingly.
- The intuition power of orange and the intellectual power of yellow will help you in dealing with the nonverbal aspects of the interview.

Starting a New Job
- Before setting out for your new job, cleanse yourself of all negative vibrations with white.
- Use green also for cleansing, which will allow you to let go any resentment or anger that may be lingering in you.
- Wear blue to communicate effectively, and to be clear and honest with the people around you.

- Wearing green will stimulate your heart chakra and help you to be open and loving to the new people and situations that you will be coming across.
- Meditate with a yellow candle burning, visualising your happiness in the new job.
- Your mind will be sharp and alert when you wear something yellow.
- A red string around your finger or wrist will act as a reminder that you are safe, strong and powerful.
- During the first week, burn an orange candle at home.
- Also during the same period, wear something orange to help your intuition steer you towards joy and wisdom.

Accepting Abundance

- Abundance is shown by means of money, happiness, love and self-fulfilment.
- Whatever makes us happy, in turn, makes us abundant.
- Be grateful for the abundance in your life.
- When you visualise yourself as needy and in want, the universe will instantly respond and leave you in abundance.
- Wear white on a daily basis to remove any negativity in you, especially during times of change and unrest.

- Use orange and purple to ehance your intuition and find your higher self.
- Use red and blue to execute your thoughts and communicate effectively.
- Keep white and red carnations in the vicinity to absorb negativity.

Success Map

- Map-making has been beneficial to many people.
- Make a large map with your photo in the middle, surrounded by images and affirmations representing your desires for your personal future.
- Keep your map beside your office desk, charting out your course, and this will help not only you in your job, but will also serve your organisation, energising and empowering everybody in it.
- When you make your map, be sure that you don't hold back yourself or restrain yourself in any way — cut out from magazines and newspapers images that you want to bring into your life, including important words from headlines, and paste them down onto the map; you can even draw or paint; just let your imagination take rein — see, how beautifully things turn out for you!

Colours of Health

- The feeling of being one with yourself and everything, gives a feeling of happiness and lets you know that you are well-connected.
- For proper healing, it is essential that you are open to the idea that colours can heal.
- A doctor can surgically remove a cyst, but he cannot remove the vibration that caused the cyst to grow — only you can do that by balancing and cleansing your energy system.
- If there is an imbalanced, your negativity manifests itself as a fear which again manifests itself in a physical way, like the appearance of a cyst.
- You can programme yourself with affirmations or authoritative statements like, "I feel really good!"
- An ailment develops when our general energy system becomes feeble, and this often takes place due to an emotional strife.
- You may become exhausted when you feel you are not getting the appreciation or emotional support you need — understanding this can help you handle issues of the heart chakra and unconditional love.

Colours for Healing Physical Ailments

Red :   Reinforces physical energy; helps cure anaemia, constipation and listlessness; helps alleviate common cold, flu and bronchitis; strengthens the reproductive system; aids the circulatory system.

Orange: Helps cure asthma, bronchitis, common cold, lung conditions, allergies, epilepsy, growths and menstruation problems; helps in digestion. Relieves muscle strain; boosts the immune and reproductive systems; aids elimination and gallstones.

Yellow: Helps bladder, kidneys, liver, spleen, cures rheumatism, diabetes, and piles; helps in mineral assimilation; aids in the breakdown of fatty acids and starches; good for digestive problems, stomach and constipation; promotes ulcer healing.

Green: Helps cure anxiety and exhaustion, ulcer, asthma, hay fever, back disorders, colic, laryngitis, malaria and piles; activates the heart, immune, pulmonary and circulatory systems, the thymus gland and general healing; aids assimilation of nutrients and regeneration of tissues.

Blue: Helps cure colic, diarrhoea, epilepsy, skin rashes, jaundice, headache, inflammation, and laryngitis; healing source for children, aids the function of throat, mouth, oesophagus, teeth and thyroid, affects the vocal box and respiratory system; helps prevent baldness and cataract.

Light blue: Helps cure acne and anxiety.

Ice blue: Helps in healing burns, cures fever and nausea.

Dark blue: Helps cure allergies.

Violet: Helps cure cataracts, alcohol poisoning, asthma, bronchitis, pneumonia, convulsions, diabetes, arthritis, lung and nervous problems. Activates the pituitary, endocrine and immune systems; helps assimilate minerals. Enhances the sense of smell.

White: Helps heal rashes and wounds; relieves cough; aids in bone-building, aids brain synapse activity, affects the nervous and skeletal system.

Health Essentials

The three principal essentials are controlled breathing, meditation and yoga.

These are the bedrock for spiritual practice, gifts that we can use today not only to remain fit but also to prepare our bodies to receive colour energy.

Breathing

- Breath is important because it connects us to the present.
- The present cannot be conceptualised, it can only be experienced one breath at a time.
- The moment we start thinking about the present, we are no longer in it, and it is within this moment that all healing takes place.
- Concentration on breath is therefore very necessary, and so always be in the present.
- This technique of breathing in colour is especially useful for healing physical conditions.
- Determine the colour that can help your ailment.
- If possible, assuming that your area and surroundings are clean, do this exercise outdoors, or sit by an open window.
- Start off with deep, rhythmic breathing.
- Imagine the colour you want to absorb.

- Breathe it in as coloured light.
- Your thoughts will transform the energy of the air you are breathing in.
- As you breathe in positive energy and expel negativity, you create an atmosphere in your energy system that is open to the vibrational effects of colour healing, because your energy is flowing freely.
- This leads you to a state of being with a higher vibration that allows you to transcend guilt and blame.
- Your breath will prepare you to receive the colour and thought that will conclusively heal and change your life.

Meditation
- When you do deep breathing, you allow your breath to set into a relaxed rhythm of inhalation and exhalation, eventually leading to meditation.
- Start your meditation with five minutes a day, slowly building to fifteen, and then half an hour a day.
- Allow yourself to be soft and gentle, and live an eternity in the increasing gap between thoughts.
- It is in this open space that you will come to realise your true nature which is divine.

- In a deep state of meditation you can experience both space and time as illusions.
- You will realise that everything is connected, that nothing is separate from you, and nothing within you is separate from any other part of you.
- As you connect with your universal consciousness, you will begin to accept your limitless potential.

Yoga
- Yoga is a system of exercises that soothes your internal organs and effects the body on a physical level.
- Yoga will help you know yourself and understand the reasons for your deeds.
- It conditions your mind and body to be receptive to subtle energies, especially colour.

Healing Others

1. Before the commencement of healing another person you need to ground, protect, cleanse, and balance yourself.
2. You can also cleanse your aura for better a effect.
3. Always be open to moderate changes, if required.
4. Trust your intuition and inner wisdom to guide you in the process, in a way only you can do it.

Grounding Yourself

1. Follow the exercise given on page 23.

Protecting Yourself

1. Visualise a white light forming a protective bubble or layer around yourself.
2. Since intention is everything, repeat this affirmation, "I will not accept any negativity, I am protected by universal love and light."

Cleansing Yourself

1. Imagine a rainbow dousing you, from the top of your head, through your body, and passing out of your feet.
2. Burn an incense stick to cleanse yourself and your surrounding environment.
3. Soak in a bath with two cups of Epsom salt in a tub of water.
4. Loosen your wrists and shake your hands up and down for a few moments.
5. Before and after healing the person, say to yourself, loudly if possible, "I am releasing all negative, unwanted and blocked energies."

Balancing Yourself

1. You can balance your male-female energies (see page 55).
2. Visualise each chakra, starting from the red root chakra, spinning thrice to the left, then thrice to the right.
3. Declare to yourself that all your chakras are in balance and harmony.

Cleansing Your Aura – A

1. Stand straight, hands by your sides, palms facing in.
2. Slowly begin to swing your arms forward and backward in tandem.
3. Slowly increase the arc of your swing.
4. You will begin to feel as if energy is being massaged around your thighs as your hands swish past them.
5. Once you feel this, gradually decrease your swing until your arms come to a halt.

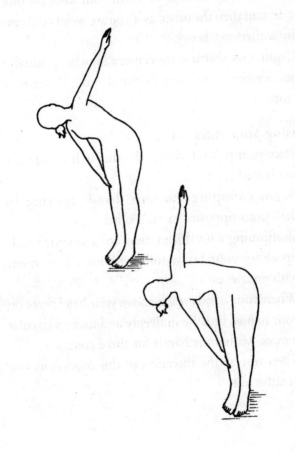

Cleansing Your Aura – B

1. Slowly bend sideways to touch your knee on one side, and then the other, as if you are weighed down by something heavy.
2. Begin this shifting movement slowly, gradually accelerating, and then finally slowing down to a stop.

Cleansing Your Aura – C

1. Place your palms facing each other in front of your lower belly.
2. Begin chopping motions, hands moving in directions opposite to each other.
3. Continuing with this motion, to raise your hands up along your body, following each movement with your eyes.
4. When your hands reach above your head, eyes on your hands, breathe in deeply and make a circular motion with your hands for three counts.
5. Then reverse the direction of this motion as you breathe out.

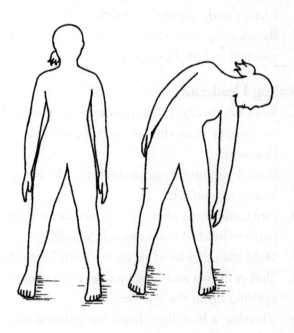

Scanning

1. When you are fully prepared for healing the other person, you have to find out what he needs.
2. Allow your hand to drift lightly and freely over your friend's body along the chakras.
3. By allowing your third eye to see into the body, you will feel the blockages.

Healing Headache

1. Since blue is anti-inflammatory, it is a good colour to project into the person's head, who has a headache.
2. Start by grounding, protecting, cleansing and balancing yourself.
3. Hold one hand about six inches above from the person's head, slightly toward the side.
4. Hold the other hand six inches from his forehead.
5. Shut your eyes and imagine a dome over your head, opening up to the universe.
6. Visualise a blue light from the universe entering your head, flowing through your arm, and firing out from your hands into your friend's head.
7. Soon your friends headache would cease.

8. In case you are struggling with self-doubt about the efficacy of this experiment, the other person will have a different experience, and you may have to refocus and start again.

9. You, as a healer, will probably find your hands heating up, an indication that your energy is being channelled directly into your hands.

Colours for Dressing

- The colour of our clothes and accessories have a great impact on how we feel and how others perceive us.
- Blue reassures while violet communicates a spiritual side.
- A white top gives a picture of purity and freshness.
- A red dress may show you are ready for a party.
- The choices of colour that we make are usually instinctive.
- When our body needs to be stimulated, we are drawn to certain colours.
- Sometimes we end up buying lots of clothes of a particular colour due to a temporary craving, only to discard or forget them after a certain period.
- A less expensive way would be to buy small items like socks, hankies or underwear.
- Then give yourself a colour energy shower.
- Feet being active energy conductors, wear colour socks of your choice to stimulate the particular energy chakra.

- Yellow gives you a lot of confidence, and is also an anti-depressant.
- Since colour is energy, your body assimilates energy from the colours you are wearing, into your chakras and aura.
- The colours of your surrounding environment and also of what other people wear, affect you in certain ways.
- When you stare at a particular colour and focus on it, you will affect the vibrations of your chakras.

Loving or Hating Colours

- We have strong responses to colour which reflect our needs as well as our past associations.
- Someone may be drawn to a particular colour, probably because they identify it with something or someone they like.
- Someone may be put off by a certain colour, probably because of some childhood association, or some unpleasant occurrence.
- When you have an aversion to a particular colour for too long, you find yourself limited in many ways, and sooner or later you need the full spectrum to run your energy system effectively.

Unflattering Colour

- If you feel that a certain colour that you need to wear will be unflattering, at least visualise the colour.
- Thought is the most powerful vibrational remedy that we have, and by visualising the colour, the energy flowing in your body will have therapeutic benefits.

Colours You Wear

- The best way to get an infusion of colour therapy is by wearing coloured socks and undergarments.
- Use yellow for work as it stimulates the intellect.
- Green will always make you feel happy and by strengthening your heart chakra, you feel love.
- Wear white or purple socks or keep hankies of these colours for elevated spirituality.
- When confused, always wear white, for white symbolises purity and clarity.
- Blue is ideal for confidence and calmness.
- A deep burgundy red or pink can be comforting and make you feel more at ease and more connected to love energy.
- White enables you to appreciate beauty in everything.

Colours for Men

- If you wear a suit and the colours to choose from are tan, grey, brown, black or blue, the best be would be blue which increases your ability to get through to people.
- In a stressful and highly demanding job, blue can help to restore your balance, and be expressive and communicative.
- With blue as the primary colour, incorporate other colours too.
- Select an appropriate colour tie (red would be fine).
- White shirt or white underwear is good for work as white implies new, and new denotes opportunity.
- Tan is very grounding and good for a relaxed earthly feel, and for promoting logic and reliability.
- Cream signals an inquisitive mind in a positive sense.
- Khaki and olive, stimulating the root chakra, imply strength.

Dressing for Work

- To be logical and articulate for a meeting, wearing blue can help you communicate effectively.

- Wear red and yellow for confidence and assertiveness.
- For a job interview, ensure that you have blue for communication, red for assertiveness, and orange for creativity and sociability somewhere on your person.

Dressing to Go Out

- If you are shy or inhibited, wear orange to stimulate your sociability and lift your spirits.
- If you are nervous or ill at ease, wear green to balance yourself.
- Wear blue to feel assured and confident.
- Wear red to attract attention, for red is vibrant, sexy and electrifying.

Colours for First Impression

- You add colour by way of accessories to whatever you wear because you want people to sense that you are a balanced person.
- You could use blue accessories for seriousness and confidence.
- Use gold and purple for spirituality.

- Pink and green accessories radiate love.
- To be assertive, use red.
- Use yellow for happiness and a studious mind.
- Always follow what you are drawn to, remembering at the same time what colour energies can be used up to your advantage.

Wearing Black and White
- Though black is a neutral colour does not let anyone know how you are feeling, it does promote change.
- Since chaos and change are always a part of our world, the black colour energy sustains our ability to cope with it.
- If the black you wear has no other colours to go with it, do remember to wear coloured socks or underwear.
- White will help you to cleanse your blocked energy and negativity.

Colourful Environment

- Our home is where our families and friends spend maximum time.

- It is a haven, a place where we can sleep, relax, entertain, meditate, plan, etc.

- Consider what kind of a house yours would be — simple, spiritual, gay, relaxing, etc.

- Begin by creating a pleasant environment for yourself.

- Clear your house of clutter, which lowers your tolerance for others, and prevents you from radiating your inner light and joy.

- Do not hold on to possessions for sentimental reasons, as this will only promote stale, stagnant energy — release and let go to allow flow of new energy into your life.

- Be sure that the objects around you are meaningful to you.

- Use incense sticks to cleanse the house regularly and welcome fresh energy.

Colour Choices

Red

- Use it judiciously in the interior, as it evokes a powerful response.
- Red in an entrance hall or dining room is fine for coziness and intensity.

Orange

- Orange is commonly used in restaurants, as it stimulates the appetite.
- At home, it needs to be used sparingly.

Yellow

- Your study room or work area can be painted in yellow as it is bright and uplifting, and it stimulates the intellect.

Green and Blue

- Bedrooms are best painted in blue or green for promoting relaxation and sound sleep.

Violet

- Violet is ideal for bathrooms.
- It is also good for bedrooms, as it stimulates dreams and spirituality.

White

- White symbolises a spiritual quality, and hence needs to be balanced with pictures, plants, crystals and mirrors.

Options to Painting Rooms

- If you do not want to change the colour of a room, just paint the door or window frames.
- Solarise the room with transparent curtains.
- Wear the colour you need.
- Do colour visualisation.
- Do colour meditation.
- Have a colour energy shower.
- Keep plenty of flowers in the room.
- Use coloured sheets and pillowcases.
- Sleep with coloured crystals.

Colour Guidelines for Specific Rooms

Entrance

- Since first impressions are important, red can denote excitement and promise liveliness within.

- Blue reflects a family with strong independent opinions.
- Green and pink symbolise warmth, love and harmony.
- Yellow signifies that the family values ideas and intellect.
- Photographs of family and friends hanging at the entrance suggests a loving home.

Living Room

- Warm colours are ideal for this room.
- A deep burgundy will give a safe and secured feeling.
- A burnt orange shows sociability and sensuality, and helps bring conversations to an intuitive level.
- A blue room will stimulate conversation and soothe the nerves.
- Green-blue combination suggests loving communication and relaxation.
- Brighten the room with paintings, flowers, cushions, vases and table covers.
- Plants create better energy flow and aesthetics.
- Crystals stimulate and promote conversation.

Dining Room

- Blue, violet, muted orange can stimulate honest conversation with family and friends.
- Deep burgundy, deep violet, green, or a burnt orange encourage a more romantic or fiery mood.
- Coloured votive candles give the room a magical light.

Kitchen

- To encourage positive energy, choose colours that are warm and friendly.
- Bright colours like yellow, orange and red will support interaction, conversation, congeniality, and activity.
- In case overeating is the problem, then select subtle colours such as peach, apricot, coral, etc.

Bedroom

- Do not have anything too powerful which may create an imbalance in the energies.
- Light blues and greens seem to be the best choice.
- Light an aromatherapy candle that has essential oils in it.

- Lavender balances and relaxes, and so would be a good choice.

Nursery

- Yellow, white, pink and red are enticing colours, but use these colours sparingly till the baby is eighteen months old.
- For an infant, pale pastels for the walls are ideal.
- Blue is a healing colour for babies and children.
- Pale blue and its vibrations subconsciously act on the infant, helping in communication.
- Splashes of pale green and pink promote unconditional love from the beginning.

Children's Bedroom

- You would like to promote balance, self-confidence, and the intellect, but respect the kids' innate instinct that guide them in their colour choices.

Bathroom

- Blue is a relaxing colour, but avoid dark blue as it promotes depression.
- Light colours of coral are good.

- A plant or crystal counteracts the energy that gets drained with the water being flushed.

Study

- To create a relaxing and stimulating environment, use yellow as a dominant colour.
- Blue is good for communication and calmness.
- Splashes of blue and white will keep work pouring in, and avoids its becoming stale.
- Keep books around that you enjoy reading.
- A painting or drawing will promote creativity.

Office

- Warm blues show a relaxed atmosphere conducive to work and dark colours create chaos and distraction – use cool blues and greens and also turquoise.